MW00489249

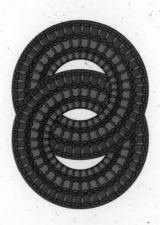

Eyelevel

50

fifty histories

Eyelevel

50

fifty histories

Christopher Matthews

CavanKerry ◈ Press LTD.

Copyright © 2003 by Christopher Matthews

All rights reserved.

No part of this book may be reproduced without permission of the publisher.

Library of Congress Cataloging-in-Publication Data

Matthews, Christopher, 1955-
  Eyelevel : fifty histories / Christopher Matthews.-- 1st ed.
    p. cm.
  ISBN 0-9723045-1-7 (pbk.)
  I. Title.
  PS3613.A845 E94 2003
  811'.6--dc22

                          2003018735

Cover illustration: Juan Genovés, *Focus*, Staatsgalerie Stuttgart, Germany.
Copyright Prolitteris, 2002, 8033 Zurich, Switzerland.
Photo of author by Lorenza Campana.
Cover and book design by Peter Cusack.

First Edition

Printed in the United States of America

CavanKerry Press Ltd.
Fort Lee, New Jersey
www.cavankerrypress.com

For my mother, Ina

Lost father unkempt, sweet sherry on your breath,
regard me from the green seat near Departures,
    I had to be your son;
bless me and these long wings, retard my fall.

Daughter and son, still stumbling up the beach
still wet, just wave, I'll know you, watch the sea
    enchain in foam my shadow,
wish me a living shape escaped above.

Dearest, o waiting ox-eyed at Arrivals,
known to me crease and ripple, something strange
    you've kept for this time, surely:
fracture the Alps and plant us living there.

Dear space and haze, last name, which I've forgotten,
prepare your hunger, something has to happen,
    the secret table's laid,
a consequence is stealing to the feast.

53. Now as there is an infinite number of possible universes in the ideas of God, and as only one can exist, there must be a sufficient reason for God's choice, determining him to one rather than another.

54. And this reason can only be found in the *fitness*, or in the degrees of perfection, which these worlds contain, each possible world having the right to claim existence in proportion to the perfection which it involves....

56. Now this connexion or adaptation of all created things with each, and of each with all the rest, means that each simple substance has relations which express all the others, and that consequently it is a perpetual living mirror of the universe.

57. And just as the same town, when looked at from different sides, appears quite different and is, as it were, multiplied *in perspective*, so also it happens that because of the infinite number of simple substances, it is as if there were as many different universes, which are however but different perspectives of a single universe in accordance with the different points of view of each monad.

58. And this is the means of obtaining as much variety as possible, but with the greatest order possible; that is to say, it is the means of obtaining as much perfection as possible.

Leibniz, *Monadology*

CONTENTS

Foreword by Sydney Lea   xi

1   The fin de siècle Muse   5

2   Ga-ga   7
3   Male Nurse (Private)   8
4   Systems Analyst   9
5   Site   10
6   Downpour: Hotel Balcony   11
7   Handmaid   12
8   Rep   13
9   Solicitor   14
10   At the In-laws'   16
11   Nanny   17
12   A Retrospect   20

13   Divorcee   23

14   William Cowper   25
15   TEFL Teacher   29
16   Uncle's Rudge   30
17   Terrazza   31
18   Sclerotic   32
19   Martinis   33
20   A Break in Bergamo   35
21   Jerusalem   40
22   Machinist   41
23   Printed   43

24   Child and Mother   47

25   Aphorist   49

26   Inside, Outside (1912)   50

27   1916   55

28   The Post-war   56

29   The Task   57

30   Private View   59

31   Emigrant   60

32   Reconstruction   61

33   Vice-consul   62

34   Grand mal   63

35   The Selfish Giant   69

36   Rendezvous   71

37   The Quest   72

38   Catching Up   74

39   The Magic Mountain   78

40   Partner/Carer   79

41   Children's Writer   80

42   Wino   82

43   Life of the Mind   83

44   Husband   86

45   Wife   88

46   Poet   89

47   Wild-fire   93

48   Neptune's Shrine   95

49   Kindly Light   97

50   The Legatee   98

FOREWORD

Christopher Matthews and His Monadology

Every so often in my life, something happens that persuades me of a benign fate's supervention. Thus, in 2001, having taken a teaching job for a semester in Lugano, Switzerland, was I thrust into the company of Christopher Matthews, one of a small clutch of English teachers on the faculty, one of whom I knew not a thing – not a thing, that is, except that the fellow fancied himself a poet.

Matthews and I actually shared an office at Franklin College. Each of us now recalls with some humor how, just after our first meeting, we agreed to swap some poems. How, alas (or so we thought then), could we not?

We bore our little packets home, each man of course with the profoundest fear that what he was about to read would seem at best disagreeable and at worst simply inept. In either of such cases, our time together in that cramped office would surely feel a lot longer than a mere academic semester.

I was far, far more more than simply relieved when I looked into *A New Life*, a chapbook published locally, in Italian Switzerland. Relief was crucial, of course, but it quickly ceded to envy, and in turn transformed itself into nobler feelings: profoundest admiration and gratitude. Here was a writer after my heart, one whose command of canonical Anglophone poetry was patent, but also one whose use of great traditions – especially of the dramatic lyric – was sui generis. This Matthews was (and remains) like no one else in contemporary verse. His attraction to narrative values, basics like character and setting and even plot, while reaching back at least as far as Shakespeare, likewise struck a chord with me; and yet those narrative impulses, along with the mouth-filling language which bore them, appeared so fresh and virtuosic as to seem all but absolutely new in my experience.

I grinned from ear to ear in my rented house.

By way of Christopher Matthews's poetry, and of the personality that evidently informed it, I felt a liking for this younger man that stunned me by its immediacy. Literally overnight, I found myself joking and gossiping and whining and celebrating with him in a way that I'd ever done only with two or three friends I've known for decades. How was it possible that all our enthusiasms and dislikes so coalesced? How was it, say, that we revered both Pope and Wordsworth, that we'd long been passionate afficionados of jazz, that we were equally inept at anything mathematical, that we thrived on the telling of stories?

Eyelevel is of course full of stories, though they tend, a bit like Browning's, to insinuate themselves rather than to proceed by annunciation or by plodding, seemingly real-time recitation. That is, they come at us obliquely, a matter crucial to Matthews's intentions for his book, which, so far from being a random assortment of American-style 'sensitive' responses, is indeed a book – coherent and, as the French say, well made. Every poem here, however brief or long, is radically dependent on point of view, even when that point of view is apparently autobiographical; the angle of vision represented by the poet's 'I' here, like every other angle in *Eyelevel*, is not only a means to subject matter but is the fundamental component of subject matter, and it must earn our credence. In poem after poem, it winningly does just that.

As part of the epigraph from Leibniz indicates, Matthews's over-arching concern is precisely to demonstrate the primacy of perspective, not only his own but also of characters ranging (my list is abbreviated) from wino to systems analyst to solicitor to aphorist to children's writer, characters from as far back as William Cowper's time and forward to our very own. As Leibniz has it,

just as the same town, when looked at from different sides, appears quite different and is, as it were, multiplied in perspective, so also it happens that because of the infinite number of simple substances, it is as if there were as many different universes, which are however but different perspectives of a single universe in accordance with the different points of view of each monad.

The work before you might in fact be called a 'monadology', as in earlier drafts it was.

A typical Matthews protagonist is a peculiarly homeless figure (perhaps a bit like his or her creator, an Irishman educated in England, a globetrotter now living in southern Switzerland): he/she has been moved by circumstance or need or curiosity to another nation or place or, as in the brilliant 'Legatee', back to a place once thoroughly familiar but radically transformed by time. The edginess of that character's observations is therefore all the greater; he or she is inescapably a bit of an alien, one who possesses little of the customary or familiar to soften the brute force of perception.

The unrootedness of modern life, then, is as patent in *Eyelevel* as in *The Waste Land*, save that Matthews's renderings spare us the least trace of Eliot's Olympian condescension. His sympathy for the derelict is as great as for the aesthete; his identification is equally with the IBM drone and the trained stage actor; on and on. His grasp of the great vacancy left in our collective contemporary souls by some deep and nameless Desire is as sure, as democratic, as heartbreaking as it could ever be.

So taken was I by this book in manuscript that it seemed a plain crime for it to be published, like the preceding chapbook, in a milieu where speakers of English, let alone readers of poetry in English, were so few. And so I brought the whole thing back to the United States, at length sending it on to Joan Handler, founding director of CavanKerry Press. By her own account, she hadn't read more than five poems before she telephoned me, saying, simply, "My God, yes."

Amen, along with salutations to Ms. Handler for bringing to American attention a volume so rich and varied and stirring.

Sydney Lea
Newbury, Vermont

Eyelevel

50

fifty histories

1

1900

THE FIN DE SIÈCLE MUSE

It's really as if 'good form' is what it's for.
One can't call her anaemic feeler real compulsion.
She breathes *Take it or leave it* – the task flares like a mirror
left cracked on a skip: it snags the empyrean

but only because indifference laid it low.

One's job? With this jot to picture *every*thing.

2

VERMONT. THE SICK-ROOM.

GA-GA

For me the enormous problem is this bubbling-up of feeling.
I didn't *want* the rain-softened angel from a ceiling near his aunt's,
nor his scorched eyes. There've been these months of dad's empty-lidded calm,
a downfall one's own fall, down the line. It doesn't sort with gifts of plants

– each a true beauty – nor stupid men who think their right stems
                                                from being human,
just that. Frank has a right to break his slack heart over me?
(if he *could* – that damp thing   simply is not frangible)
and so moons about like Jesus or – worse – comes on brotherly.

For a while now being round men has felt like shifting lumps of wood,
they're so heavy, and I feel clumsy, having shucked the sex-war gestures.
Not that I'm grace and lightning with the girls, but *there* I'm agnostic,
absorbed, while the god of sex rears so toad-like, hulled of vestures,

an evil vision in dried glue. Dad's crash has gone numbly along
with a general wearing-down of feelers tuned to life – we're not picking up
quite the wide wave-band of the bored. He – put bleakly – *can't* be bothered,
and I'm too happy, though I must hide this (if I'm nimble, slick enough,

small, sleepless. . .); but the tilted mirror with the bed-leg plunging through it,
the annunciation a souped-up bike sprays – wild guy scouring our green lane –
they make candor cry out in greeting, from a mouth burned bright with love,
praise the loose dice-throw of a world flailed like fall's roof-whipping rain.

3

BOSTON, MASS.

MALE NURSE (PRIVATE)

The kid's walking into doors.
Again, he can breathe a rumba.
Last night he had such mild seizures
as if, light, he could not die.

I tell her the brain has fallen,
it's bits – some bright, some nowhere.
Sounds great when he chuckles about,
slight kid with a coke, a kink, a Rubik's cube.

"Don't tell me what I'm thinking,"
he says, then fouls himself
unknown. Solo. Changed him
and he hung on my neck like reason. Had no say.

The mom calls him her Charlie Conundrum
and trusts I'm the stooge to fix him.
Midnights I want mom's fanny that sweet much
I palm her kid's bursting brow.

4

SYSTEMS ANALYST

To play the pattern of the butt-whipped clerk –
not what I'd thought the stars shone in that garden
home when I left my mom grazing the News
and breathed its last-chance blackness: otherwhere
than cinched to the latest nit-pick fate smelt then.

And mother empowered me some – she wouldn't lay
aside our due to grope the easy come
but held out long but shrivelled zestfully.
Long gone. That little word is coned like hell
in the throat, blank-spoken: Now; was plain bad business
squeezed out – "She's gone" – by Doctor. Which was Then.

Try drowning me, push, sister. Hold my tongue
– for silence, sure, but also to suck the thing –
wet to the wincing threshold. Dopes at work
breeze on about the lays they reap with bucks,
hookers. But we're *all* ass. And fat-cats fuck.

5

SEATTLE, AUGUST 2001

SITE

For days a strong wind has polished the cloudless sky
and the old bench goes unvisited: tired green, it just squares across
at bright sheeting over the new mall's half-built frame.
Sometimes stray off-cuts catch life and go spinning into the sunlight.
Rucks in the plastic draw gainly figures as tall as trees.
The air so parched and, somewhere, chill
tells us, though never so gently, *All change, all change.*

6

WRITERS' CONFERENCE, SARDINIA

DOWNPOUR: HOTEL BALCONY

I'm afraid you'll think the rain drops into me.
Well we're covered enough – and the blooms are bright like candy.
Not a breath. Only the stretched-out blues get wetted.
They don't spark the bleak evening a bit. Hope's weakest lightbulbs...

I won't gloom at you much. I'm holding off from that.
Don't you sense that Jim's quick intro fired some kindling?
You've flown in from the dripping North. Don't be disappointed.
We'll pile a great blaze to give the grave a pulse.

Let's talk until dawn – there: I'll speak with a lover's freedom.
I'll ask you – you seem so brave – not to grasp and quail
when I turn out a leper; ignore the raw gape of gladness
these hours might crush from me; look past my falling:
preside, Paul – make it lock-step! – at my reading.
Ghosts wail in one key. And let's get sacred drunk.

7

DONEGAL

HANDMAID

Set down on unchristened beach with a track to make –
As if! But I can imagine it. Storm-blue water
sealing, unsealing, the jade-green gash, the suture,
the stitching of foam – Mother's gone to take a leak,

she's back. Also Dawn. Plus Angela. One rank carload,
all talking. – Not the way that tide might talk to me
running off in thick whispers to turn then walk to me,
some jag snagging the jade to flint out on the whale-road.

Ocean. They call it sea. A cold sound that is
with the *whoosh* of a wave in, ocean. You couldn't say
that they want me along. They need. It's mother's way
to take buddies abroad and a third for service, gratis,

"my true girl." I'm not that. They don't know *what* is.

8

B&B, BRISTOL

REP

I'll remember it in a minute,
less than a minute, time
enough for *all* that, *must* be:
plain see – when I've laid the day –
All icy as is, numb tit   but,
fucked, mine own. . .

                        Not the guy's whose lacy fat-boy sneezing
quite fails to displace me, arcing through the room,
nor one Madge Patterson's, who is wanting me to know
            (a wish ain't knowledge, fuck-face)
            "A cold is anyone's, a cold is Nature's" –
Midge? Nevertheless, I'll need you both to go –

When they leave
                        the room sets like lard, cold fat-clapped bacon;
next a nebulous thing, that ghost,
                                    frayed off, frail gone.

9

SOUTHAMPTON

SOLICITOR

Sunday evening: time for a dank sonata,
marshy bass, treble gulls clattering
inland, in a mob.
                    Inventorize the gracenotes
as zones of gnats, quavers as water ouzels
quick on their shanks in the gauzy freshness of margins.

Marginal now, the mildest print in earth
something flowing could, even for a moment, find distracting,
let the music gloze your history and heartbeat.

But tomorrow, my tomorrow, *prestissimo* variation,
will the audience love you? Where is the conductor?

§

Each morning is wrangled out in duty
though the light is frank and fallen on bonnets and windows;
starlings provide like angels for themselves and kin.

What does a journey say when undertaken
daily? The traveller is opened to instruction
by weather and light, each road an immovable feast
though shivering gulfs are made, unmade, by salt, by sun

endlessly at the end of the street I work on.
Appointments with light – can they be kept
                                as a decision in the flesh?
Why did the old lady's frail hand, veined and ringed,
falter? Will I ever get home

if home is the sun's thumb-print on the horizon's
blade? But to guess the questions lends the answers
the hairtrigger swoop of starlings undulating
on bruised distance evenings stretching out

and leaves to us their gift of roosting sadness,
trembling hands, the mortal tremolo,
and orchestrates the dusk it all becomes.

MODENA

AT THE IN-LAWS'

The trouble with goat? It's just with its being so carnal,
and at Easter of all times. Tough. Rank. Hanks of scapegoat
and the quivering leg that, kinked to be springing off,
gets brayed by the tether, welted. There's the grape-shot

dung, part squashed by the trapped and prancing hoof,
an exquisitely tilted cube that's dense as resin,
thrall to the spastic thigh. . . —Suppose it looks morbid
for *capretto di Pasqua* – a mouthful – to let all this mess in,

these qualmy associations: but the brain keeps spinning,
spooling its dream-compounded loop of truth;
a glass of the red might chase the scorched-hair taste out,
bread cover it up – but the goat flails on, aloof.

NANNY

Thunder last night, relief like breaking fast,
with the first clap I hurried to the window.
The tower block on the coast was smoking,
the streaming fire-escape was darkly stained.
Populous air, the sky banging out reprints.
Feeling the cold (I had only my dressing-gown)
I felt this night much easier for the dead.

Here is the proof this town has swallowed me:
each morning I check from the window with open hand
and it's always there, the spill of light rain.
Perhaps the damp accounts for their speechlessness.
To be candid
                    (some small consolation)
no friends yet
                    but the parrot, my present
a child paid in the simple exchange of hands.
The wings are painted in light ochre with a pinkish tinge
like some of the old buildings in Ravenna –

Still,
        that is all a long way off
and will not return, like certain sunsets, or the song of the woodsaw.
I tell myself complaint is commonplace

but then the sun or moon undoes me.
In Italy a cherub, here the fiend is *haste*,
though on buses, when the window-flap is open
far at the front, upstairs, the grey air dances
reconciled, for the time. Oh then
                                        to breathe is easy.
How do they matter, so many little shops,
long sideviews up the sidestreets, hollow bells
(one per church – dong – like punctuation)?
It means something, somewhere, to someone, and to me
too, with different meaning. All the world!
From all the world I chose this homelessness.

And Vera writes that poor mad Gina died,
which I had lately come to suspect:
        I could no longer hear her.
When her mind unmoored from the wharf of its occupation
the dumb tide, always running,
        plucked it away.
To meet such terror every day;
to sleep
            as her heavy mother sleeps
– like water
                sinking into water –
and dream, a pool her image sways within:

Better to keep away from them,

                              or get away,
as nuns to their seclusion, each white soul,
to the heart's purple incense and trapped echo
– myself the same: although my crazy brother's
buried too deep in hospital to haunt me
he's mixed in with the rest,

                              one part of why I came.

12

LONDON, 1938

A RETROSPECT

1

We marched. There was the night of a moon so drugged
with lustre, and with such a spreading ring,
it wafted our dead leagues past their sprawled equipment,
the trash of their luck, each stiff, diminished thing.

2

Night graced spoiled flesh with a pie-crust glaze of silver
so the dead weltered sweet; moonlight smote the air
like freedom, the heart's desire; a new life trembled
in time with the front-line guns, and gloried there.

3

By tramping we dodged the trenchfoot – there'd been drought
for weeks: still the fosse was crusted-over mud;
pistoning calves and thighs worked breathing wonders
on a bog-sunk folk whom deadlock long had battered.

4

Come peace and Versailles that forced march blanched to myth
but meant life from the first – breath, much beset by ghosts:
the cankered dead dogging our toiling bootsoles,
cool backroom brass, their gas, those moiling hosts.

DIVORCEE

He mops at his eye, late March, where it's liquefying,
near the nose, that allergy,
                              then stares hard at the poster
freezing a small-girl choir, without pathos,
                                   hard, the bane being pollen,
hence the oozing and kitchen towel, no hankie, the cheap torn stuff
        pranked with daft slogans
like 'snort' and 'rump' and 'sneeze'
                              and a repeating white-heat moon.

1800

WILLIAM COWPER

i

Noah
enlarged from the
ark, Jonah

when he came out
of the fish,
and myself

from the good sloop
the Harriet.
Unconfirmed

but unconfined. Surrounded
with water
as if I had been surrounded

by fire. By night. Prove to me
I may pray,
and I will pray without ceasing;

praise too,
even in the belly
of this hell.

This is strange –
you will think me mad –
but I am not mad,

most noble Festus,
I am only in despair. This house,
I lived in it once,

but now am buried in it,
and have
no business

in the world
on the outside of my sepulchre. . .
Such are my thoughts about the matter.

But don't be alarmed.
I ride Pegasus
with a curb.

Passed. Alone. Athwart.

Passed longingly
from the sphere
where the stockdoves

rejoice
in seclusion,
curtailed by the starlings' commotion,

caught
to the
curtain of rain,

the birds' squawks
and cruel beaks upraised. . .
Saw with regret the

laburnums syringas
and guelder-roses,
some of them blown,

some on the point of blowing.
Still
there will be roses,

jasmine and honeysuckle,
shady walks
and cool alcoves,

and you will partake them with us. . .
a latitude of boughs
upbears us

yet
innocent
of blood.

iii

As in Dodona once –
a seedling, hid in grass;
then twig, then sapling. . .

Settling on thy leaf, a fly
could shake thee
to the root, now tempests

toss not. But the scooped
rind, that seems an
huge throat, calls to the clouds

for rain. Gloomy, into gloom
of thickest shades
from auburn nut, an oak

which I often visit, one of the wonders
which I show
to all who come this way,

and have never seen it.

TEFL TEACHER

Don't your bowed heads forget you? Mine is aching.
We're sitting here, we're talking; nothing's said
that isn't laundered, each of our quiet loves

lies sleeping. Are yours far? Is each heart a boat
the great wind of absence unmoors
on hot nights? On nights of long rain?

Danced into fervour by some vaporous tongue
or soothed, soothed by love's cloudy sleepsong
– how often? Yes, and now? Your fingers whisper

and unintelligible verbs ripen. Pile them here.
They are my dry feast for tonight. Then wake her up, thirsty.

CORK

UNCLE'S RUDGE

He won't retrospectively denounce it.
You saw him sometimes, but from the edge.
How he licked carefully the tobacco-paper.
Addict. He called them Rudge.

"Where's Rudge?" he said; or, "Good Rudge."
He won't remind us of it. You came down
to Rudge quite finishing him. Uncle. Give them up.
He won't say it now, so I've said it for him.

17

TERRAZZA

The light is fractious with coming storm.
He strides up fiercely to her table
toting a chalk-white cigarette
that frays into grey; lets drop a rumbling
greeting.

The scattered diners are tensed-up for rain.

She returns her "Hi."
It is blank, ironed-out,
one perfect blue sky.

My dwarf coffee holds all she's hidden.

That eye-sized depth (a *ristretto*)
forms the dark core of thunderous boomings

but from the way they lean their heads together
over a guide-book, the two grey napes
have found ease in their dead-end seesaw,

so I sip to them. No real thunder.

SCLEROTIC

Out of kilter –

one, the gap-eyed friend
'bi-polar' and crushed (new drug),
inert, hailed to our table;

then *two*:
the lanky parasol
ill-set, plumed with tottering pigeon
(one leg?), five steps away

where *three*
the flossed pumpkin head
of a toddler wobbles rising from its buggy
on clambering palms.

No *four* – or maybe the sentence
(*Till death*) served teetering

so one rises, palm on table,
reflecting *Everything, in the end, yes, leans on air.*

19

MARTINIS

Two ants on sun-lit canvas,
en face and reverse – an awning
Jane's hauled over us now the Spring's in
and the six-legg'd creation's turned on.
I'm bored. One grows observant
when the company's audibly ticking.
All my life I have wished the guests gone.

Jane stares, acts mild, abstracted,
I gaze myself into the fauna.
Perhaps we'll get left alone.
Meanwhile there's breadth in this awning.
One side there's only an ant,
the other zigzagging shadows

which one sees are also ants
signing just their most salient features

such as speed, and being very small,
a toy's aimlessness, its hysteria,

non-meaning that leaves a life weightless
as love does, but cancels the music,

and a caged thing's restlessness,
and the TV's man-eating flicker

but still ant, hard ant, trace ant

– they keep asking such *boneless* questions –

like a word both shadow and stone,
like a face half stone, half shadow,
like poor love, so rocky-lipped
its best eloquence is to goad the first guest to go.

20

A BREAK IN BERGAMO

i

Sky-mounted stoneways, windows untouchable, rooftiles,
and Dan come in loose-pressed trousers with all his boats burning,
having just lost Joan. I've found him a room in the lower
– the *bassa* – half of town. And I came to the station.
Now we're out for a walk. He squints at the flaring gold man
marking *alta*: the guy's far-slouched in human losing
but the saint, erected like noon, twins the stone March sun
and they're blitzing Dan so both eyes are running water.
Ah, don't think he's crying. He's blinder and deader than that
and spouts to lay Spring's first dust.

                            By his side *I*'m crackling,
electric, and eat right up the stratum down
from that sparkling apex – a plum-dark band of loping
viaduct-type brick arches with humping couple,
rapt anoraks at work so sharp it scars
the skittering eye. First thought is that hollow Dan
needs shielding from this, so I lunge toward the *hush*
alongside us, a flock of cyclists, one twinkling body
hiss-whispering on, and gone. "They've a uniform
now" says Dan, half-hearted – hurts just to mumble –
sleep-walking the grief. I don't ask him for his meaning.
All sense is leaning, long-term, on the climb.

It might be thought tame, the silent funicular,
and its riders do stand stiff, they do grow still;
their hearts blur with the sliding upward and their eyes lose bite,
wane blank as the world swings open and a lost horizon
strides behind haze. Dan's stupefied. If not numb
I'm ringingly absent, lost to clashed flashbacks, gross
dolts toting flags, arm-bands, the dogs of Party
we came on below. Straying, but thick with purpose,
in town for some clockwork rally, kids pimped for uproar.
Fuck them. I look at Dan. His jaw is working
and the slack of an eye-pouch pulses. To see the eye
side-view makes it bulbed glass and the blank of this
round the sad-ox blue gaze – which looks clean past its function
and, seeing, sickens – is all that lights the profile:
there's a ghost of weak hue like a hand at one high window
glimpsed and the figure's gone but you'll bear its blight
in mind. "We're here now Dan." And the cab has touched *alta*.

iii

There's a song. We sit so high it's all but spent
in the ocean of air. Back from the Gents to this terrace
I'm watching him slouched as if to fill a glass
from his slung lower lip; one trembling elbow threatens
his usual *corretto.*

                Those sectaries – way downtown
bull-roaring, up here a blade across a taut drum
tit-tittering – he's clean forgotten. Yet he remembers...
Impossible to speak. The glory at play
below helps out, inventing contemplatives
though for Dan only the ranked blind pregnant windows,
these heights outfacing zero, still stand possible:
the man never shifts his head. What he sees is unblinking.
I'm looking away, my face engorged with sight,
the town a bright gravid haze alive with gleams,
the absolute sky x-ed over with leggy jet-trails.

iv

Threading the jostled lanes
Dan's holed, each turn a manoeuvre:
the guy needs a tug, he is shipping
that much water... I'll need to drift
wide – then, in his eye,
wheel and hope he'll catch on.

Time for the *passeggiata*,
its inevitable black hawker,
its arm-led, splay-foot cripple,
foil for the supple stroller,
also Dan's bleak totter:
these triangulate bold noon.

The square glitters with confetti.
Hearts beat steady in the sun.
A chair for Dan. Kids *jump*
to launch the bits of paper,
hopping ferocious hops
teeth gritted, punching nothing.

This scene of feral gladness
repeatingly avoids
belief, just as its weird
expansiveness escapes
embrace – or recognition.
Their time is too real to know.

Backing the brave, the breathing
stands a four-square *campanile*;
two-thirds of a dome rounds out
this background, really foreground,
and bottoms the living smile;
their bell spells twelve o'clock

and I shuffle on with Dan.

v

Right at the end we find the smothered path.
Dan starts up, empty-bodied like a garden
Pan, his face swelled out to vinyl smoothness.
The martins, the light aircraft seemed our own,
companions, godlings level with that terrace;
they're joined now, as we leave all breath beneath,
by stepped and vine-dressed slopes one swoop removed,
skied neighbours richly sculpted by the young shadow
and gold-dark grainy light. The dark-bright cypress
across fathoms of air; the minor emerald mountains
perturbingly complete, low, dryly wooded,
strung out toward the far hazing; the utter silence
wombing hard, urgent birdsong – Dan finds a troughed stone
and sinks, head frayed, hands lolling, the tears of solder
falling or like fat stones, or like mercury slowly,
as if he were oozing the vestige of that death
and she'll robe the whole hillside and overwhelm our morning
right out to the hazed *campagna* widely flashing,
to the cast of wild gold that stakes the effaced horizon,
to the sleight of the sun-god striking the hidden line.

JERUSALEM

Pearl was a girl with a mug so cloud-rack mobile
she'd take you right through *Exodus* inside one sentence.
She levelled her wide-gapped gaze – secure – but then
as the éyes rólled the grín yáwed, curving on,
expelling itself. Wait! Next breath, Jerusalem:
besieged, of course, and falling.
                                    Lost. Pledged afresh. . .
Incline that cycle steep through every heartbeat.

How much of this was 'charm', how far sheer *fatum*
you couldn't say – though borne on by compulsion:
that much was sure. But did guile tweak the outflow,
put a curve on it – dint spate, like a rhino blinking?
I'm interested as I'm interested in fountains,
say the ones which lob white water high, sustaining
a frittering peak for months: more than most heartache –

*un*like Pearl's breaking, deliquescent smile.

MACHINIST

I've always admired – well, envied – Mel's richness of feeling,
just that sometimes the 'inner life' is the Doncaster bypass
– you're not happy, natch, but it *has* you –
skin like tarmac and the infinite boom of traffic
jammed in your nerves. That's when I can really hate:
it's a too-short step for me. For her it's unreason,
it's what bird-song and funding food aid should make shiftable,
love leave – impossible. Well, but it sometimes mugs me and mine.

So this tiny event has stuck: eyes dragged to the left
sharp skyward, a mini fit, because of the dense
black wobbling blob that twangs right past my eyebrow,
seems gone, then like a rock strung on elastic
– big bite sized – zooms and slam-bams a reach away.
A few seconds, but time enough for the brain to start asking,
then bang! and the headlong eyes plunge into blue.
Clean gone. Left me jolted, stung, stock-standing, clueless.

It was Easter, that's understood, and pretty much frozen
here, whatever the lush leaf your way's doing.
I'd been having a dry time too, all facts and spastic,
so to feel as if some truck had caught my collar,
yanked, and let go – it left me flat bust, forlorn,
post-coitus: fright, as if I'd grazed a cable
and barely escaped a frying; been dropped, vibrating.
What note did my skull sound out? There's that ominous

overplus, when you're full of it, giving forth,
and nothing comes back from the vacant concert hall,
not even an echo. That's when I started thinking
what if I look as hare-brained as I feel
but no workers are out at 10 on Wednesday morning
and really cars aren't like persons. There was one tree
a few steps along; some dark-leaved, year-round type
with a hanging branch so it almost scraped your forehead

and a gaping drab flower suspended. At the heart of this –
like some high-tech press to speed things in the vineyard,
dug into the tangled organs and smeared with yellow,
methodically treading as if it was treading water,
sealed off in a life-term dream – one large black bee,
not buzzing, not thinking of flight, just the steady mill-work
of legs and pulsing body, set like a token
or sermon on something, and life where there was nothing.

I didn't tell Mel. Look, I haven't told *you* mate, really.

23

PRINTED

Somebody doing something, a tune, a bold trickle of water,
then running, raising red dust on the road from a here to a there;
a shout in the street, young rain, Paris, the withering stink of wet fall;
boys glad-handing then flashing away; a fast car's fat-throated cry –

Around that time Mac's tic had its tooth in me.
I'd widen my nostrils, inhale, let my lip lift, 'sneer'
(with no meaning); sort of taste myself; and this reeked of him
but I'd catch my face at it with reference to nothing.
In those blank-soul moments this phantom moved in on me.

It started in France. The man's broad rotating tongue,
chub lip, they had no place in that brighter Beyond
but would always, right after the wince, rise up sharp before me;
having loaned him my nerves, you know, the glimpse cut keenly.

What say the super-subtle? That a mere acquaintance
couldn't borrow my mouth without some blood-secret say-so
– which bespeaks the false-bottomed suitcase of the self?

But this was 2-D. There's no 'depth'. A far different force,
less touted, advancing on dove's feet, ruled and rules here.

I mirrored the man as a stone bleeds repetition.

All the glittering things, all again: unchoosing, each flare of the pinwheel.
Time's trick of slick-dipping the dipper: black water wreathes in the well.
– Fatalities churning like dust,   in constellation,   in suspension,
and a touch-blue gunpowder cloud fizzing static over the earth.

CHILD AND MOTHER

My tongue is small, it cannot weigh
the syllables I must obey.

These words will be your own in time;
they will forget that you were mine.

I know that I am yours when night
remembers, and I wake in fright.

Dear, fright is all we come to know;
when love's forgotten, fear must grow.

GASTHAUS NEUBAD, 1908

APHORIST

The pine-trees are dryly *there*, and the paper *here* –
my pen rustles across it, or the bright skin of my hand.
The two mix to a scratching shuffling. What looks a pale bonfire
has just burst inside black branches: a bird-cage for sunset.
Now – incipient thing – the first bats lash, whip-crack past.

Then who is to say this life's not friends with me?
– though no sister, still less buck lover. You rise at the husky
shiver of dawn, your gut hollowed with expectation,
the waterjug crashes its ice douche like numb rain,
a hectic first light red-fevers the stolid doorframe.

It's the pain of desire, it's these new heels' blade-edged scuff,
the blustering tread that rips dust from the bald hall carpet;
that volleying of the stuck door, flung back too rudely,
lids cringed at the bitter stillness vast outside.

INSIDE, OUTSIDE (1912)

i. Hansi:
Living above the Bahnhof Café Theatre

We dream at an open window. In the morning
it's joy to chastise dim snow from the counterpane,
a dust of it. Big winter, bristled beast,
snorts in the bedroom, twitching icy skin,
and we drift and semaphor and flail from shadows,
strike rock, wake as the first light storms the ceiling.
She's dozing now. I've roused one drowsy nipple
when Friedel knocks. She barely peels from sleep
but I'm up and treading shrinking into tweeds
the night has hung with frost – and how their weave
scours one along! with Friedel always leading.
High hayseed shoulders span the corridor
always two steps in front, our skins burn yellow
and he sways ahead. I'm playing *Der wilde Mensch*
and already the tragic grimace scalds my mouth:
"You leave me; you all leave me; I breathe leaving"
– I *try* to say this *in*haling – "The bloody spike
my heart's become..." The panelled corridors'
dumb wood, the low-watt bulbs, irregular,
wide-spaced, the crape and wheezing of our progress –
all breathe the dark note I tune my Wild Man by
and which Friedel, as Stage Manager, *should* approve,

though I feel in the anxious oaring of his palms
on the steeper stairwells (he won't trust bannisters)
this avatar of Hermes *pale* and *cringe*.
It's close. An angelic hubbub from the green-room
hangs dancing somewhere deep and hale beneath;
the floorboards buzz with it and Friedel slows,
clutching my arm. To advance we have to stoop
where the warped wood of the ceiling bears us down
and sombre walls constrain – so tight, fat Friedel
must squeeze behind me. Single-file, my face
thrust ignorant, a prow, bold at the gloom,
we huddle along, champing our jaws in madness...

These regions are spent and ritually dusty
and the sofa you bump against explodes in dust;
the chairs and beds and windowed cabinets
which litter the passages are richly hung,
all's twilight, but now and then a dirty loophole
flares in a stairwell; Friedel, straining up
on tiptoe, out at the swimming edge of things
and filmed with grime can glimpse the veiled canal
and maybe a stuttering tram or motor car
but, without a sill to grip, he has to drop,
and his fear supplies the crowd's broad leaden glare,
his hammering heart its vengeful mute applause
till we shuffle on. Far off, the whole cast is howling.
To leach from the shuddering lustres of those footlights
this dirt and dusk – it suits the paradox
our *Intendant* is torturing to birth.

ii. Peter:
Commuting along the Bahnhofstrasse

The trams lurch from a dead stop to wild speed
almost without transition, so they press you
just once, but with finality, hard against
the slatted benchbacks. Pinned, you pass furniture
houseless and coped with snow, left standing out
past scavenging, stone voices in a yard
bursting across the spines of frozen mud
a drayman's cart churned up one day of thaw.
The city's veins, irrevocably frozen!
Like an isotope, I merely circulate
lodgings to work, but though my daily round
is sealed and dumb, I think I've found a friend.
I caught him one zero morning where he sat
bolt opposite, absorbed, a black-backed book
held high up wholly opened on his flat
supporting hand, his parched eye quenched at it,
angling the pages like the holy water
a stoup steeps in its darkness, fouled and fair.
But *you* know you can't too closely scrutinize
even the most abstracted brand of stranger
if he's facing you, you have to patch him up
from glints and all the broken jewels of looking:
dark coat and tie, a frog's thighs, harsh face grey
and ready to yield the sad dirt of the grave
when rubbed with a finger; unsweetened as unfresh
the lustreless black hair that drank the oil
and still would rustle; tendons on the neck
slack in the too-large collar; puckered shoes
like larvae, greatly shone, but worn and thinned –
When he got off the tram had then to wait
for many boarders, whom he slipped between,

then cleared, with a lizard's ease. He wasn't tall,
walked on his toes, wore narrow, blade-grey trousers
that showed off bulging calves, and altogether
discharged a dry galvanic energy,
flame stalking the brumous length of the Bahnhofstrasse.

Needless to say, I watched out from then on,
hoping to catch him, though not for days and days
did the low and cap-like hairline reappear.
(It is notable that that density of hair,
low-browed, goes with a dense, *metallic* odour.)
Once more he sat opposite. He had the book
and as he read drew out between the leaves
torn strips of india-paper, pale and fine,
and seeming to bear the faintest trails and traces,
lead-silvery memoranda. Glancingly
I noted his pearl-grey fingers, how they tapered
from knuckle to tip, too smoothly, how their sides
shone like the slabby flanks of animals;
but mostly the pencilled words intrigued me then
and how these seeped a tender luminescence
on the scraps of paper. (I felt it might augment
out of strong daylight, held in cupping hands.)
He rode with me until the selfsame stop
on the cobbled roadway, by the grey canal,
and left with the selfsame forked, unheeding fleetness.

Now I've watched for the man, all achingly, for days,
and if you ask me why – I hear you asking –
I can only say, because I chose obsession
as another might choose to whore or play the market.
(We drudge at the office, hollow with a hope.)
So I dream of him, or picture him, awake,
with an edge that cuts the heart out of the morning,
and it's most his unfathomed room I long to probe,

the space and slanting light my thought has worn there,
a place which, woken in, brims one with hunger.
Does he live on the Bahnhofstrasse? Dark and carven
the massive apartment buildings range along,
unlit by the tarnished mirror of grey water.
The raised and lowered blinds fulfil a code
you read as the tram sheds drifts of livid sparks
and harshly beats the stone: two blank, one down,
a flash of shirtsleeve, a woman alone, marooned
and backlit, high up, extending shadowed arms;
and always, at every stop and step of sight,
the pathos of some distance. Like a sky-
backed bough, that world rears black and quick beyond me.

THE SOMME

1916

There's grit in a faith, rude strength – but I'm too feeble
not to love my life, Christ perishing; not to clutch
this vanishing, maybe foolish; not to flinch from God's love.

And the blackness of our trench – can't shape it my pew,
dream the fetor incense, the smashed limbs *corpus Christi* –
Help me, I can't believe... But to die like a man,

that animal, man; but to lose my shining lady...
– It's here at the end the word, though fallen down
in blood, returns, a lost thing rent from home

but found where great rage has scoured man back to pilgrim.
The comely sound sweetened his quartered mouth:
"water," he moaned – I don't think I'd have touched him

except the word christened him and turned from muck
to man this Jack, this broken, dirtied baby,
a soul splashing in death's wet throat, all gape and gargle.

– Which is funny: his little fever shakes and shakes
and I'm sponging it (with filth): as in a mirror
the clay convulses right to the horizon.

THE POST-WAR

1

An avant-garde pigeon, a stunt, a flare, a gage, a rogue sniper's sundown,
a convulsing sheaf of feathers with all the chic flipness of a glove
tossed at the Opera. A ring-dove, maybe. An icarused flight to prove
spirit of gravity and the dense earth will win out hands down in the long run.

2

A shot bird won't make the large-mouthed papers: their brows are
                                        stamped with '1919'
as if that befriended us, made a homestead in the wild mud our time's become;
with the late hostilities and since, a generation finds its 'doom'
– like 'new cultural developments' – rich grist, and the bent mill-wheel keeps
                                        on turning.

3

There's a vast coolness around the cold green of that larch dancing
                                        with black-caps:
they go piercingly about for the dazed, filmy flies; they chirr their wings
to unhinge them into spiced gloom; they twist and dangle, salving sharp pangs,
devouring ranks of the ghost ephemerids: their tiny lust strip-mines the gaps

4

in a black market of needling dimness. Why is it this makes us weep?

SILS MARIA, UPPER ENGADINE, 1922

THE TASK

Frau Siegen, sitting across from me over lunch,
eyes open, but drowned within – she was seeing nothing –
some dead weight had claimed her: it had turned her haunches stone
     and splayed her horn feet, some plummet.
It had emptied her eyes. The line of the upper lip
was dry against dentures, feeling the drag within.
Her mouth was stiff as a carved mouth on a temple,
     the set lip a lizard's footstool.
But looking too long has made my heart a boor.

A great absence had noticed her, and then *I* noticed,
but the real thing is action – he hadn't prepared the moment
so it came on like labour: the man stopped, he dropped stone down,
     and his legs (the poor shoes much scuffed)
got thrown about at those angles beyond arrangement.
Just yesterday. Under the starved blue of this sky.
With a dead wind from the snowplain. At my galled feet.
     My breath was fleet, harsh and calm,
my face a bright mask, as I knelt on the ice to save him.

But at lunch I found my hand shaking, very slightly;
vibrating – the daylight flame of aftershock
that can make stone quiver but burns beyond form or feeling.
     The excessive Fräulein Hess,

as part of the guesthouse custom of a round-table
arrangement of diners, presses the cold meat's claims,
presents a potato, prattles. Her faint moustache
        renders the food disgusting
and I creep to my room, where I'm happy to dine on water...

The just, surgical word bares a motive's million sinews.
It can feel like enough, the blade broaching the raw volutions,
the blinding weave of the dancing-master's foot.
        Only action, though, flays them *deeply*:
when I stand at that downstairs window my pleasantries
are aimed to flush out their drives, cloak mine – to lure
each smaller self from the tranced mob of its Person,
        have lust flex itself alone,
free rage, then let it drown in sips and silence...

– But a break, now, from bad air; rest from that parlour
awash with its inmates' cycles, digestive, social,
the twisting of pique, the tweak of the need to 'go'
        (to where *I* make sure I *don't* go:
here's my chamber-pot; there's a cairn of my frozen turds
a walk away). When one sees a bird skim the snow
– keeping the contour, cleaving, till a dip
        opens – that moment owns us;
then we're lost by the nothing left when the bird's clean gone.

30

BERN, 1942

PRIVATE VIEW

Christ, and don't these bastards talk! Now the light's gone bone dry
the yard starves back to two dimensions, slate parched by a puddle
the colour of engine oil; this blinks in one corner
while another (can't blank the muted drivel of 'views'
loose behind me) hoards, in patience, its gruel of black leaves.

An inheritance. Also the quietly striving trees
that lure the grey-brooded eye away from the hum
of the show – some Klees – and launch it across a wide valley
– stick river, municipal buildings, then clambering villas –
till it founders blank at the sky, that wide disclaimer.

As if domed in a bell-jar. Here, the all-pensive man
– saw him how many years ago, but the mind takes pictures –
might have angled his naked head, and with thinking fingers
tried the weight and pain of this terrible still air.

31

LONDON, 1949

EMIGRANT

I ask if the light turns lemony at the horizon.

He says no, more a kind of gold paint, but really diluted,
then – the salesman's touch, when he thinks I look disappointed –
"Our big thing now: this live rose from Galilee."
Flame-new, it loops from PackWrap on the tallboy.
Long thorns curve out to guard the absent bloom.

The chap's suit looks wet. The colour's like the stick sulphur
shamming dead in our school lab, held inert in oil.
Jaundiced with smothered blazing, the mere air meant combustion.

A dry-point of burdened Herzl primes the room.

32

BERLIN—DOVER, 1953

RECONSTRUCTION

The system of rewards and penalties
jeeringly comes to a head
until, between dodge and scut,
it locks and sets and shames us.

That's why I've had to come broken
to this jostle of chalky breaths,
not knowing what glue might unlame me –
that's why their necks are white judgments.

This England: fistfall of rain.
Raw mattress. The twice-sapped teabag.
They breathe and a day yaws out,
leans from them: they make that window.

So our place is the room, not the view,
and well back of that surd The Nation.
The floorboard the heels strain up from,
the sill the palms beat, *that*'s homeland.

33

PORT SAID, 1953

VICE-CONSUL

Trees – spiky, one flat as spatulas – indent the horizon,
then the usual blue a small plane wanders from
and, downward, man's paths and pits: the crude half-built wonder.
It's as dad says – never *should* have crept from home.

Granting him right, still the first charm is things' strangeness
– then being stranger to that. High. Just as the sky's estranged.
Complete. I feel too bluely to keep starting
from their scatter of bits: am not, enough, deranged.

But the chill height leaves one courting! – where's the breathing
of *that*? The dead stone which flickers on my lawn
I could whisper a secret to with as good reason,
betray the sky's blank-page wisdom. Grave?

Forlorn.

34

GRAND MAL

i. 1960

Some days, the hair's-breadth absences fall teeming.
When it's black, you've been clapped on both ears, and the sound-world

is blooming

coming back is to the dance of light's density,
you feel up-beat and hell – lost a dime and found a dollar.
Mom says, "John, have *all* your props been knocked to firewood?"
and I wake up minutely ringing, the same aspen leaf
but another attack-worth's weaker.

Foul pillar of fire

and rolling pillar of cloud, in clinkering two-step,
sway me down to the night street, numb, but I need an airing
so swing out, my scalp alive to the prickling heavens.
When I reach Lakembaya Street and its long arcade,
well-roofed, I feel less bescalpeled. A steeper darkness
adrift on my left is cellar-flaps blank open –
the eye picks them out, not seeing, but as they sap it,
night hungering on.

(I *sense* there are clumps of sleepers

in the right-hand doorways.)

Cheese, good gorgonzola,

bolted dust and crust, as found – I can't remember
how many days ago. *Yet I feel no hunger.*
Something hauls my look left again: that seam of light

– stepping out on the silent roadway, a breathing stillness –
shadows one guy still wild awake. To see the rich gash
in the narrow façade is food, and the coffered ceiling
luridly underlit, ridged green and gold,
a lizard effect embossed into the blackness
like the pang of high game

                              – then, highest, the brain of heaven,
raw starlight. It chases me back toward the arcade,
dancing over a coal-hole. Heaving, the fit gets sprung.

ii. 1990

Perhaps I should never have been in Africa,
it brought the worst seizures on. It also augmented
an old foppish lust for the raptures of night walking:
sensibility's spy, my fits came star-fermented.

Then there were all the howlings heard from home,
especially Mother's; strange, that maternal outcry
echoing under an upside-down Orion
post-episode, as if her rage deranged the sky.

Of course the whole trip's attributable to trauma,
the first blade-touch of serious illness. Not easy to handle
at twenty, falling void before the advance
of your future, that serene head-severing angel.

35

THE SELFISH GIANT

And the giant cried "O   who has done this to you?"

too late,
>   though warm tears were shed;
>>>   though the goodnight kiss was warm.

Then decades, a bitter fluid. The man's life has scrolled by.
Elsewhere, he rolls his blank head on a pillow.

The flawed bedroom glass is buckling a jet-trail.

RENDEZVOUS

When the heel of a nail hauled half of my shoe-sole off
– I was haring across the room till the sharp clack stalled me –
my reserves dragged to zero: no pair of sound shoes, no money;
this counted, but I was hell-bent on achieving the window

where a pausing, intent blue sky was silently flexed
and, palms to the frame, raised up the two mortal holes
at which something, not eyes, slept staring – erased, re-forming –
the ghost of our doubleness,
                              the strange mild friend.

THE QUEST

i

No name. A brief sharp-tailed thing. With what grew a real span
of wing to unpack – from a thin band of weightless gilding –
it wreathed tinily from my thumbnail; just like the man,

was there, and then gone. I couldn't locate the building
either, nor where he'd shown me its shadow from,
hoaxed a roof (gauzed by spray), spun a life some salt wall was shielding.

Half charlatan. But though he couldn't open the stone
book of the place, he mirrored one drifting feature
in his mystifications: the town's oceanic tone;

so to stand with a thumb raised, gaping after a creature
for an orientation – well, his blather'd half-started that,
and set sea-surging homework. None done. Find another such teacher

to 'steer' me? – no. And no 'voyage': I must pace it pat,
must trudge to reach the dark things that lie stark beyond me,
the blank step through some gateway, the door – hell, the *rat-tat-tat-tat*. . .

"Hello. Who are you?" – or, "how" – the vowel caught up nowhere,
as some stones on the beach here hang between clear and cloudy;
and hard to make out how high they've dropped it from,
or quite when, and if from that steeply-gabled absence
let into the roof at a hard, angelic angle,
no colour – the eye, tiptoe, lips its frame of green.

Tall house. Not the kind of ground there where you're thrown down
and a *dies irae* sun extracts a stub shadow
– makes you precious; and there aren't those roaring veils of foam,
the one, lasting gale that blasts in the black-bright breakers;
facing the house isn't facing that kind of furnace
though an ocean might set you up for their scale of things,

the height of this house. Funny, the steep-up garden
you glimpse at the back – the tough lawn, the few hanks of clover
thrilled by a hunting wind – it's what grips you first:
secret kingdoms and mouseholes, *Alice*, that kind of thing
– first stage. Then I took to walking the long way round
from where light sinks into the pores of beach and sea,

letting drop a late dream of order for lurching sightlines
snatched from over their back gate, jumping. *Abashed at being seen,*
still unhinged by that shifting question, I scrape to the wall.
Far above a stuck something shudders, comes harshly free:
from the flung-up window a figure surges way out
and – caught, I just look – waves, wind-torn and asking something.

CATCHING UP

i

The dispassion of that back,
setting the skull to scan high dusk-drab windows;
   the ash stucco of each frontage,
badged with the worm-casts scuffed up from warm sand
   on dead days with his sister
decades ago, when they coupled crime with boredom,
     lust to sly fright;
   when they cast the slow die for life
and sex always came foaming in, their own clockwork ocean.

   A stage. They sprang beyond it.
Eventually one great fear gripped lapsing life
   and their swoon found proper footing:
they lunged for their clothes, surged on, two comely youngsters
   only slightly anaesthetised
and on fond, non-fondling terms. Though a bit cut out
    of each still twitched
   it would have been vile to notice
those limbless fractions clasping in the tide.

Half a lifetime, then his letter.
I'd had no idea through all our years of tones,
    of terms, of glazing friendship
– never seen this town. And yet we'd been close as water.
    Never met this sister. Now
life breaks blank out, but me stalking up dumb behind him
        feels pantomime stuff;
    legs braced, the huge head thrown back,
he looks mad, eyes nailed to the true north of one window.

I've hit a funny place
this trip back to my dawnings.
Some crust is breaking up.
I sense that there are things
opening up and out
inside me – things just starting,
the hum of cell division,
a region where each haulm
stands whole, disjunct, and true,
articulate as *Oh,*
deep kin with all the rest.

My just-pubescent sister
grows from the grey earth
squatting to pee – no drawers,
hoarse fingers plucking soil
gaily as she squirts,
squinting, non-committal.
Her look acknowledges
I lust, *But that's for you.*
Myself? It's a good piss.
She shivers and the stink
winds heavily about her.

Blank pane. But now a light
flicks on. The unshifting shine
and absence of all shadow
itself sets off the budding,
the crowding, a belly-scooping
delight. My lips are drawn
tight across my teeth,
await the unsteady Now,
hold back a wave of spit:
I taste, I am, this grimace.

So it's sheer embarrassment
when Mark shows up. I'd phoned
hinting and set a date,
says he, then scrawled a letter.
As we turn off for a talk
the light shies from the window.

THE MAGIC MOUNTAIN

This is a place of recuperation, in the snows.
The luminous autumn sky giddies and rises.
Its knuckles of stone and blue are bruised in interknitting,
they secure the horizon to itself. Our flesh is gentle.

Afternoons a white stupor breathes from heaven.
There are blue nights when every heartbeat is a kiss
the breast shakes with. Everywhere the ice
mirrors your single face in sheets and flaws
and shows it cloven. The trailing sack of day
is stuffed then with resilient abstinence.

I can't say how we came here. Half-numb, burning,
your face wears a pied mask of ice and fire.
The hearth in this high lodge flares. A gaunt window is open.
Our smiles blaze and freeze, cold air, cold flame.

PARTNER/CARER

It was bliss to ally myself with her club-foot graces,
    with her tremors so peeled and clean;
she was clumsy, but overfed in all the right places,
    and liked this to be seen.

She might trip, she might clatter a cup – you could feel her groping
    inside, then beyond, the lesions;
M.S. had turned her movements mild and sloping
    as a Hindu cow's: us Friesians,

we were four-square black/white flatbacks, ornaments
    unstirring; she twinkled by
misaligned but tiltingly rich, subliming torments
    to gapped grace, dusk's barred sky.

Sunsets: they're what it takes to do flushed justice,
    that plangency. Plus lust.
I'm still chest-deep in life. Her death hints that my trust is
    dumb. Yet breath is trust.

CHILDREN'S WRITER

Now I've dug up paper and pen I'm as empty as morning,
that skull-round of winter sky, hollow and clunkable.
It's a stillness life's always grimly twisting toward,
light's idiot smile, mesmeric: so I grin the stiff grin
of the Cheshire cat, as weightless as erasure;
in default, day sets *that* down, but it's vanishing...

What nonsense! The trouble is, it's my only meaning.
With children the ticklish thing is to bag the bright theme
but grown-ups wish cobwebs, words: I'm not up to adults.
I could write a Part 3 for *Alice* – original
but crutched-up by greatness, dead Dodgson redone, made 'modern',
a live hand in the haunted action. (They'd still finger *you*,

reviews...). I could botch some starved, millennial *Snark*.
But to kick the old props away, take a chance on ruin –
well, I'd need the material. When you think you've got it
that dead weight drags the clockwork from the mark,
blanks the light you'd planned on laving your point of view in;
life invites the wild Boojum down – bad art garrottes it...

Stepping out then, wrapped like a doge, mind peeled for the word,
the dense clove sunk deep in the dead lard of late morning,
for an essence all premises, I feel the flat wind
– it's *ice* – rebuff my eye; chill trims my squinting;
light flashes forth deadpan tears. Just like the vast Alice
what I'm lachrymosed by is downright, plain as stone;

this impasse, though, kills the story: viz 1) the bleak fowl
pronged onto that branch, cold-welded starkly upright;
2) the rage of the perpendicular; 3) daylight moon
crescent and badge-like perfectly aloft
white tree and hieratic bird; 4) the rune that all these
lock into, impassible –

                  Art, strictly numb!

WINO

They set me to learn the red thread on my cheekbones
and, tinily-bezelled, the grapeskin of the wave;
three times I was tried and then they deeded me
His kingdom, furious with signatures.

Where I crouched down, a crawfish in a curve
of dirty earth, to sleep, the sea's foot slid
up rough against me, amorous of understanding:
so the blind carp require the thinking cave.

I walked abroad to read the dumbish birch,
its meaning stoop, its ill skin scribbled through;
thumbed the dropped leaf; I got the gorgeous page
blueblank behind, steadfast, and by heart.

But (Father of detail) creepingly, a wren
as small, as sensed, as doubt   winced through the farc-
ing green: with subtle rustle though the branch
hung bland; with pronged impertinence of arse.

LIFE OF THE MIND

i. She

When merchants, bright sailing ships crowd in the skies
John looks up – has been long staring in his broad lap –
his mouth lengthens and tightens; the light glums from his eyes,
he's erased, the throat thickens as if a burlap

sack were being stuffed with goods sour from the Levant.
The hum trade makes inside him drowns the neighbours
but he greets the fraternal kingdoms of aphid and ant
and now swifts and black circling crows, enskied with his labours.

*Every*thing's tool or fruit, he tells me, and how
even knitwear, our cloudy glassware, bears "glints, impalpable."
The researches have morphed his life: every gesture's prow
ploughs Atlantics of print, freighting sand-grain souls – unscalpable,

micro pilgrims, their spating silts up all our spaces.
Not to make him sound mad, but imagine a room full of flotsam
and struggling limbs, Madeira in casks, gaping faces,
beeves – bound slaves so dark-packed that it rots them;

set there *husband* and *wife*, lay-figures in pyjamas
whose words, dead ritual now, bore him back to the terrace,
mint tea, two salty crackers. That brain – driving llamas
(alpacas?) – turns bow-legg'd peasant and I drive to Bury S-

t Edmunds for lunch and a glance not world-historical,
meet friends, try to breathe. How wooden we've become!
– I've learned that it's the insensate's the diabolical.
Shut up in thought's walls the inner life's a slum.

ii. He

Research: a state of suspense. I've set proud my markers
and wait for events to show: shade zones, map tensions.
There are three still trees attendant where I'm working,
a beech, a birch, a maple. All it means to have courage,
haunting through these, I feed on – which means I don't 'have'
and is why, maybe, I dog joy limpingly,
accumulate like interest, brace for a crash.

The big wórld, the great blazoned chance, the top of the tallboy
back home where I glimpsed that gift, unreachable,
meant for Mother – its veiled sharp touch when I swayed beside it
on a chair on the top of a table, the tilting ceiling,
the crash – oh Christ, and all my fabrications
sprung taut across the ribs research has found
plus her car's noise fading for town,

                    all feed the world's blaze.

HUSBAND

Here's how your sleep went:

knees bent,
the coat from chin to thighs –

your legs in flannelish grey trousers,
your feet in quilted slippers –

as the neighbours seeped through the wall,
as our awkward son stumbled in, and out –

with your head tilted, like a ledged gull's-egg
(which I must regret) –

with the fire low,
for economy,

dear,

you came,

between comfort
and the slog to bed,

on a colder passage: that stir
of the coat

told me.
And I wrote this. Secretly.

No warmth in it.

WIFE

There are rims, bowls, cups; all mine. And there is blood.
Rich, and rich.
       Sunlight, which all think blameless, and woman's blood,
sulphurous. Where's purity?
            I don't make myself clear.

I should, of course, regret my vanished freedom
openly, but sir, you find a girl's tongue best *on yours?*
And as for speech! A woman's speech is yes or no
ultimately? You think so.
          For my children,
I can't regret what they have done to me.
They are quite beautiful, in their measure.
             I am their mother.

POET

Last night, after a screaming, blue-
arsed flight by junk and limping rickshaw
I faced the Muse: "Your tongue's too slick, you're
fluff," she whispered. Is it true?

The lines come, but not dark, not deep,
nor tidal in a moment's room:
they scum the drowning-lake of sleep
and you can't wake up too soon.

I woke this morning to a mist
of rain, a taste of table top;
I thought I'd take a verse's step
– alert, somnambulist;

and walking, mindful of the time,
balancing view and destination,
window-shopping for a rhyme
came late, to Brighton station.

Infinitude of ingress there
balanced by egress infinite!
So many comers – inertia's bit
stretching the mouths, and fear,

fear in the eyes, wincing, smiling,
pleading the freedom of a journey,
greasing the bars with charm, beguiling
fate's cheap attorney.

Away then, quick, the bit loose and
bail's terms all fixed: One summer's day –
granted, but leave as bond the grey
flecked shingle, the gritty sand;

and leave behind the sun looped
and shivered on the meshing salt,
sea-grained skeins in light steeped,
the dim, archival silt;

while over the trainclack (as under the light's
elastic life webbing the water)
runs the pounding tidal order,
the blackness, the swinging weight

the ear knells best, for poetry
is confluent with time,
and feels beneath the grassy sea
the wasted dancers lean.

47

WILD-FIRE

The vast world pressed on us its lovely weight,
the flank of a grand sow, and we were half-way smothered.

We knew it was all for the best, that it was meet, even to amputation.

First we were disposed by thick sure clumsy fingers,
then stowed hunched against heaving bristles, in the stink of
                                                uncommuted safety.

So what is this new-born hard wind,
this whoop as the trees fly, all going off like fireworks?

48

PENSION ATLANTIQUE

NEPTUNE'S SHRINE

A man with a folded butterfly between two fingers,
the wings pinioned, the toiling legs free, going nowhere
– snatched it that way from a branch, now he's stiff to keep it,
that's the *feel* of the guy; look, we haven't shared a word.
He comes and goes so tight you'd need to pierce him
but it's more than certain he has bliss locked up,
keeps a shape for his mortal eye, one shining loophole,
a mercy of perfect light doused in the dark.

I've been here just long enough to start to notice
the shape of his world – the raw islands pushing up
out of the surface guest-house life sustains –
and its future, staining his flinching irises.
What I haven't been able to get the measure of
is where love fits in. You'll say, well, work it out
and I'm endeavouring, indeed. Fate doesn't gossip
but put it all down to a glimpse through closing doors
glimpsed through his closing door, which swung to noiselessly
with him tranced at a cupboard, back to me, spread arms closing,
slow-closing its double doors. A thing turbulent
and lovely, riding his tweedy slumping shoulder,
he was sealing away – an oil of such surging freshness
it transfigured the heavy pausing bachelor
as he turned aside, as I winced and skipped off sideways.

So I've dodged to my room; I'll *try* to unpack the parcel;
it isn't as if I'd seen King David dancing
but that flash of a painting, the sense of windy seacoast
off-stage and huge, in the foreground the blank square bunker
with doorway punched in – it led *down* – then, lifted high
up into greenish air… a *some*thing, a statue
gesturing into the unseen miles of water
and fused with the hissing, salt-soured atmosphere,
the gauzy light – the spoiled cream of that smooth
stump bunker –
                    it all swarms together: but somehow the picture
endures as a whole thing, snatched beyond his profile
then gone, shut up, with its blank-eyed keeper turning,
bowed and transformed – well, 'saved'… That's not the meaning…

– I hash it together, pacing round my room –

His raw seaward gaze: the man was sick with longing.

49

KINDLY LIGHT

I've been rubbing away: it's a patch like the scuffing of plague
    or the scab that caps a winkle;
I've tried various creams, no use – as when titties sag,
    no change; or the first sharp wrinkle.

I know that women are wired to moan a bit
    when they slide into autumn glories,
to wince wisdom from watching the fall of the earth-drawn tit:
    What's Hell? – Time in the raw is.

But then 'women' is *me*, at the 5 a.m. of the world,
    not lost, half happy – laughing;
relieved to find most of the blatant banners furled,
    no sex left worth the staffing.

And saved? – the whole joys of a top-notch cup of tea,
    pangs close as pot and kettle,
thrills not felt (when you feel them) blurred and wincingly,
    struck off from the boyfriend's mettle,

but at home and sole and always – or as long
    as the light lasts: happy eye!
I'll have yonks of that looking yet; grab, if I'm strong,
    live bliss before I die.

THE LEGATEE

I've come round the long way to surprise my inheritance.
These deadweight bones, fingers of a child or an ape,
thin skin but bark-bulbous knuckles – all day I'm staring,
all day I've been scouring my palms for ancestors.
This tree where I sit – you look up for the sky
and the depth of the blue is mazed with leaves and branches.
Birds clatter there, oldest friends, and the past seethes thickly,
goaded by needling cries; when a hampered wingbeat
speaks, a dumb door swings back: *shapes round a table*
fetching out snaps some Christmas, and one dull girl
a bit aloof, big teeth, with broad soft hands
who meets my gaze and, burning, keeps on looking,
which makes *me* look and look, till we're both wild scarlet –
we shall only be saved if she drives the blade right in. . .
(Where was the judge? Where the high court of justice?
I have nothing to say. I shrug and show slack hands.)
– An empty face that wears its blankness frankly,
a bare throat, crude blouse thrown on; then I looked away;
but already housed an indelible opinion.
Later, the promenade of sulks and secrets,
fear tarnished our hearts; but first the fierce clumsy whisper
astride the black running gutter, and the thirst of foxes. . .
Tuned sharp in my shade I can ghost-taste her pulpy mouth.

One troubling thing, now I have this place to love
– and the garden alone's enough to salve a leper –
is the way the house formalizes memory.
It's hard to set up safe camp on such mined ground,
though that's half the point: just *that* it's deeply fixtured
and it's here poor father brooded, mother crept,
red ants raised earth-crumb cities – all things cumbered,
all that waits on the wail sunk in the standpipe's throat.
Trees croon to me how, at forty years of age,
I've winced home to set up as genealogist.
It's why I've upped sticks and run here, shedding funds.
(I haven't a pin. I'm 'obsessed' and drawing dole.)
– Genealogist, yes, but also an assassin:
what I have to do, when I've traced it all way back,
is obliterate some tormenting little pictures:
make all the adjustments, work out the tremendous sum,
tot it right up, reach death without remainder.
Meaning? – I'll take these items from the sequence
and wipe them out absolutely, so that nothing has been.
So that, not *as if* – feat crazy as levitation,
stunt out of the order of nature, sulphur-stinking,
blind noon-struck leap for a *shadeless* legacy.

There's a lot at stake. I'll need to move really sweetly.
Though I've tagged the convulsed events which I'm to lose
– though they're gougingly real – what if my 'guidelines' are wrong?
Erasing the raw-flesh heart of what was chosen,
the point at which all paths kissed, and then streaked away
(newly infirm) – well, perhaps that's too obvious.
There's a metaphysical angle. Take the stalled train
those years ago, winter, days sweet and empty.
I've left the hotel. I walk toward the level crossing
and a goods train approaches. Downtown's the other side.
There's a woman, a fellow guest, fat, halted there.
She'll rhyme with the train. I broach her unmeaning back

with "There's *always* one coming. Like life. Gates *always* closed"
when, magically, comes a grand slamming-on of brakes
and we both – she still hasn't turned – freeze, stormed by noise,
and the desk-clerk comes running, waving a telegram,
in his own, and perfect, silence – glad fly, glad glade –
knees lifting, sprinting an unseen bicycle,
his mouth a dropped cellarflap full of coal-glinting darkness.
Her daughter is dead (I get this in flushed aside)
– should have asked him why such news was hacked out so harshly –
and the next is, I'm through the gates, she's been cleared away,
an immortal circuit's been born: fat *Frau*, shut gates,
train, running clerk, then darkness looping back;
and how to get out from this the twisting question.

– Just one example. It's a puzzle, the hardest homework.
I step from that hotel lobby and ancient air
embalms the whole rigmarole, which seems immortal;
so love turns on its spool (is turning now...)
implacably – like lust, or haste, or losing:
the long-limbed crystal melting on her lip
in Sils Maria, when she bent over me;
stag-beetle in leaden flight drawn past the window
stark upright, a spook, the long jaws curving onward,
beyond it the eaves and attics of sway-backed Bern.
That night, how she looked at me! (I'd made some booboo)
then let her pure lighthouse gaze sweep round the room
hunting one photograph – she *had* to have it –
coarse face with its crumpled nose and cowish eyes
moving in just that insect's heavy furrow,
dredging the nap of things. Ten years ago.
If I stood up now and turned I'd find a window
low through my branches – next house, sunk in its hollow –
where another, the first of all, undressed to please me,
me pressed to the welted trunk and scalded, heavy,
first tryst of the lustful eye, till she gleamed away.

I've been sitting how long? Two hours? This place streams detail,
shades numerous as a fever patient's heartbeats;
the grass looks black-bright, the light (somehow) is *lined* with darkness.
There's a separation; a silence, posthumous...
– Hours gazing, the widening mind bulged like a lens,
and the pictures just piling in. You can't look away.
A shop window, smashed; a signboard, scorched and splintered.
Black-brightness conceives a hunched vision of smoke and cold,
a first glitter of snow. The gouged stone of some street
lifts dust around a tram's heavy, blackened skirts.
The thing's not moving. Bombed? It's been burned out.
In the foreground, two lads: they're what all the dumb angles shaft to.
One's grown and thick and he settles, facing us,
cap pushed well back, hair slathered – capable,
one of the big boys. Oblique to him, in motion,
approaching this playmate (maybe) but neither's looking,
so they seem to be dancing out the dead day's quadrille:
a smaller boy, long shorts and high-laced boots,
a cap on too, set straighter, the slack arms hanging,
high-stepping, a straight, straight back, and knees knifing up.
It really *could* be a dance, but I know he's walking,
and his friend, who's brutal, weightily gazes past him,
the hands heavy and held out front and filled tight with blood.
Crows lifting off, making black swirled contusions,
but the rest very still and the tram cold and uncoupled,
first snow in the air... Now *what* in God's name's the root
of these visions, or fits – the rich damage of grasping backward?
As I gloated and rummaged I grazed some sepia image
curled in a drawer and it floats up, claims connections?
Or the shade of another life – perhaps my father's,
a rag-arsed streetboy, mum said, in his time?
Well file it with the other nameless inundations,
and get up, fill a kettle, re-hear that old *clack* of water,
check out the sour plumbing. Lead? It's your legacy.

Sometimes a man coming home – and not to his first home,
not even to home as he now might try to name it –
and the sun is big (after weeks of retardant spume)
with its habit of joy bulged out, and up, and over
strummed blue that wide, and wider:

                              sometimes it's then
that a quaver-beat unmixes his cloudy spectrum
and the bands stand clear; then, shouting, joy takes hold,
blooded with rage. And both hands start in shaking. And though nothing can last
and that doesn't – although bliss shrivels the heart of his deal,
it's a strangler's grip. Because this light wants forever.

ACKNOWLEDGMENTS

The author is grateful to the editors of the following periodicals, in which some of the poems herein first appeared, sometimes in slightly different form: *The American Scholar*, 'Private View', *Argo*, 'William Cowper', *Crazyhorse*, 'Catching Up', 'Ga-ga', *The Dublin Review*, 'Nanny', 'Husband', 'Wife', 'Child and Mother', 'Poet', *The Lung*, 'A Retrospect', 'Neptune's Shrine', 'Sclerotic', *The Rialto*, 'Lost father unkempt'.

Poem #14 consists largely of phrases put together from William Cowper's letters and from his poem 'Yardley Oak', together with some words and lines of my own.